POV Press
Books by Bethanne Kim

Survival Skills for All Ages:
  #1: 26 Basic Life Skills
  #2: 52⁺ Everyday Recipes for Emergencies
  #3: 26 Mental and Urban Life Skills

Scouting in the Deep End:
  #1: Cubmastering: Getting Started as Cubmaster
  #2: Scout Leader: An Introduction to Boy Scouts
  #3: Citizenship in the World: Teaching the Merit Badge

Not the Zombies:
  #1: OMG!
  #2: BRB!
  #3: YOLO!

The Constitution: It's the OS for the US

The Organized Wedding: Planning Everything from Your Engagement to Your Marriage

Forthcoming:

Survival Skills for All Ages:
  26 Outdoor Life Skills
  Special Needs Prepping

Scouting in the Deep End:
  #4: Mentoring Youth in Scouts

Scout Leader:
An Introduction To Boy Scouts

BETHANNE KIM

(a Dumped-in-the-Deep-End Scouter)

Copyright 2018 by Two Crazy Boys Publishing.

All rights reserved, including the right to copy, reproduce and distribute this book, or portions thereof, in any form.

Ebook ISBN: 978-0-9849542-4-7
Paperback ISBN: 978-1-942533-13-9

Scout Leader: An Introduction to Boy Scouts is not an official publication of the Boy Scouts of America® (BSA). This product is not endorsed or sponsored by the Boy Scouts of America.

Cub Scouts™, Boy Scouts™, Be Prepared®, Pinewood Derby®, Eagle Scout™, and many other terms used throughout this publication are registered trademarks of the Boy Scouts of America. For a more complete list of registered trademarks of the Boy Scouts of America, please visit:

www.scouting.org/sitecore/content/Licensing/Protecting%20the%20Brand.aspx.

DEDICATION

To all the Scouts and Scouters who have come before me,
to those who are here with me,
and to all those who will follow me,
I dedicate this book.

Table of Contents

1. Finding Help
2. Organizational Structure
3. Unit Organization
   Adult Leadership
   Youth Ranks
   Youth Leadership
4. Meetings, Meetings, Meetings
   Leader Meetings
   Cubmaster/Scoutmaster Minute
   Annual Planning Meeting
   Youth Meetings
5. Popcorn Sales and Fundraising
6. Training
   Youth Protection Training (YPT)
   Other Online Leader Training
   Unit Trainer
   Additional Training Opportunities
   Outdoor Skills Training
   Youth Training

7. Uniforms

   Cub Uniforms

   Scouts BSA and Scouters

   Loops or Tabs

   Uniform Boxes and Misc.

8. Rechartering
9. Ranks and Awards

   Ranks

   Awards

   Cub Scout Awards

   Scouts BSA Awards

10. Summer Camp and Outdoor Activities

    Summer Camp

    Pack Camping

    Troop Camping

    Hiking

    High Adventure Bases

11. Special Events for Cubs

    Blue and Gold, Crossing Over, Arrow of Light

    The Derbies

12. Service
13. Webelos and Transitioning from Cub Scouts to Scouts BSA

    Losing Interest

    Transitioning

Scouts BSA

14. Assorted Scouts BSA Specific

    Merit Badges

    Scoutmaster Conferences

    Boards of Review

    The Eagle Process

    Order of the Arrow

15. Useful Websites and Apps

    Official Boy Scout Websites

    Unofficial Scouting-Related Websites

16. Conflict and Being a Role Model

    As an Adult

    With Youth

    Handling Anger/Frustration

    Apologizing

Endnote

About the Author

Other Books

Contact the Author

ACKNOWLEDGMENTS

Thanks to my husband, sons, and parents for their encouragement. Thanks to my parents for getting me involved in Scouting and helping me stay active all through school.

Thanks also to Bill Mayo and Roger Claff for sharing their many years of Scouting experience. Their advice helped make this a better book.

Introduction

"When a boy finds someone who takes an interest in him, he responds and follows." (Lord Baden-Powell)

Cubmasters® and other Scout leaders often get their job when the outgoing leader's son joins Scouts BSA™, quits Scouting, or moves. If they are even still in the unit, the outgoing leader may be focused on transitioning into Scouts BSA, making it hard for the new leader to get help from them. The new leader has to learn a lot, fast.

That was my experience and I know I am far from alone in it. My son joined Cub Scouts in November and I became Cubmaster ten months later. There was one (1) month of overlap with my predecessor: August. The overlap included one leader meeting, one den meeting, and one pack meeting, where I was introduced as the new Cubmaster. At that point, I had never even taken part in a popcorn sale. I couldn't remember our pack number. Talk about getting dumped in the deep end!

This is written from my perspective as someone with a lot of Girl Scout™ experience, but no prior Boy or Cub Scout™ experience and your experiences will undoubtedly be different since your council, leadership position, and other particulars may be vastly (or slightly, or not very) different. I had to learn everything down to what a den is on the job.

This short book is intended to help you become oriented in Cub Scouting and Scouting BSA. It is not detailed instructions. If you buy the e-book version, many topics have links to more information online, to read when you are ready for it. Whenever possible, links are for official BSA® pages.

As you may have already discovered, the problem in learning about Scouts isn't a lack of information but rather the immense volume of it out there. It is my sincere hope that this is short enough to get you started without being overwhelmed, but thorough enough that you feel confident in your new role when you finish reading it.

Last but not least, thanks for reading this book! Your time is valuable and I appreciate your using some of it to read my book about being a Scout leader. I hope you have a great time in Scouting!

Good luck in your new role and *have fun!* (Can you tell yet that I think fun is important in Scouting?)

YiS (Yours in Scouting),

Bethanne Kim

All Baden-Powell quotes in this book are from: www.scouting.org/filestore/pdf/Quotes.pdf

1. Finding Help

> "The Scout Oath and Law are our binding disciplinary force." (Lord Baden-Powell)

My personal experience is that there is plenty of help for new leaders, once you know where to look. A lack of resources isn't the real problem. The problem, for me, was simpler: I had no clue where to start. Another leader directed me to our local Roundtable and that was the best thing that could've happened to me as a new leader. There is a lot to be gained from the programs at Roundtable, but there is a lot more to be learned by simply talking to other Scouters. **(Scouts are <u>youth</u> who are active in Boy Scouts; Scouters are <u>adults</u> who are active in Boy Scouts.)** Casual conversations can help you learn *a lot*.

FINDING HELP

There are many different forms of help (magazines, mentoring, training) and places (meetings, online, events) to ask for help in Scouting®. This section is far from comprehensive, but these sources will give you a solid starting place. "Comprehensive" is for search engines.

The Be a Scout website is an amazing resource. If you aren't prepared for it or don't have a specific targeted question, the volume of information can be overwhelming. To give you an idea of how much detail it contains, there is one page just to define the acronyms and abbreviations experienced Scouters use, and which can confuse and confound new Scouters. One entire section is devoted to documents for Cub Scout leaders and parents. The history of the movement, safety concerns, meeting planning, values, activities, and more are discussed.

www.scouting.org/scoutsource/Media/LOS/abbreviations.aspx
www.scouting.org/sitecore/content/Home/CubScouts.aspx

In addition to general information, Be a Scout has targeted information to help units with potential problem areas. Are you concerned about multiculturalism or under-represented groups? There's a page for that. Trying to figure out what happens in pack or troop meetings? Yep, there are pages for each of those. There is no point listing everything in BeAScout.com. Take a few minutes to look and see what you can find to help yourself. BSA has spent a lot of time assembling the information. Use it!

Chapter 6 discusses Pow Wow, Scouting University, and other training opportunities in more detail in, but they are a great place to get help. Helping Scouters is the entire point of training! In addition to the actual learning experience, these events are outstanding chances to ask questions and network with experienced Scouters.

There are a lot of experienced Scouters out there, ready and willing to help you find answers to the oddball questions and problems we all

FINDING HELP

end up with at some point. They really are your best source of help. If you aren't talking to them, odds are you will end up wasting time re-inventing the wheel. The fast way to find someone with a lot of experience: go to Roundtable or a large training event (Pow Wow, Scout University) and look for someone with lots of knots on their uniform. They will definitely have a lot of experience. (The "knots" are leader awards.) Of course, others with fewer knots may have a lot of experience too. Some choose to only wear a few knots or don't bother applying for them, so don't dismiss those with few or no knots either. Ask around! Help is there.

When all else fails, or you have a truly oddball problem, contact your unit commissioner. A 5th grade Webelos in our pack broke his thigh bone and was confined to a wheelchair while it healed before he finished his hiking/camping requirement for the Arrow of Light™ (the highest award Cubs can earn). It was possible that he wouldn't physically be able to complete that requirement, so we developed a just-in-case plan with our unit commissioner. The unit commissioner brainstormed ideas with our council district executive ("DE") because sometimes there just aren't ready made answers. I certainly didn't know enough to reach a workable solution without their help. In this case, the Cub was given permission to do all the planning for a pack hike and participate as much as he was physically able.

For new Scout leaders, my top three recommendations for help are Roundtable, Scouting Magazine® (including the official blog, *Bryan on Scouting*), and BeAScout.org. Roundtable isn't available all the time like the other two, but you can contact the new Scouter friends you make there (you are networking, right?) between meetings. Getting comfortable with those will go a long way toward getting settled in your new role.

2. Organizational Structure

"The most important object in Boy Scout training is to educate, not instruct." (Lord Baden-Powell)

The national level is, well, national: Boy Scouts of America or BSA. There are four "areas" are directly under national. There are 26 regions under the areas, and 300+ councils under the regions. Each council has several districts (smaller geographical areas within it) determined by the council executive board. Packs (Cub Scouts), troops (Scouts BSA), and crews (Venturing) make up the districts. There are also ships (Sea Scouts) and posts (Explorers) for older youth, but not very many. You will need to learn the name of your district as well as your council.

Per the official BSA website (Scouting.org), a council is a voluntary

ORGANIZATIONAL STRUCTURE

association of citizens, including representatives of organizations chartered by the Boy Scouts of America™, to promote the Scouting program within a geographic area. The major functions a council performs are membership, finance, program, and unit service.

Councils guide and support their districts in promoting the ability of Scouts to do things for themselves and others; training them in Scoutcraft; and teaching them patriotism, courage, self-reliance, and related virtues. Councils establish policies and programs, and take care of administrative tasks. Districts carry out these policies and programs within their territory.

Friends of Scouting (FOS) is BSA's fundraising group. In short, dues go to national and to individual units. They do not go to councils, and councils have summer camps to build and maintain. FOS fills that void. Each unit schedules a date, normally a regular unit meeting that parents are at, when the district FOS presenter gives their pitch to everyone.

Very few volunteers interact higher than the local council. Councils own and run summer camps, develop training opportunities, and generally provide administrative support for units. Your council may photocopy flyers and other documents for your pack, upon request. This may be more hassle than it's worth for small jobs, but if you need 500 copies of a JSN (Join Scouting Night) flyer to send home with every youth in your charter organization, the unit treasurer will be *much* happier if don't have to pay a commercial copier to do it. When our council makes them, they put a brightly colored BSA flyer on the back, which is a nice bonus.

Even more than the council, most of a pack's interactions, including training and special events, are normally at the district level. Your DE (District Executive) is a paid employee of BSA and can help you a lot–it's literally their job–but they are responsible for *a lot* of units. Districts have a monthly roundtable and at least one representative from each unit (Cub Scout pack, Boy Scout troop, Sea Scout ship,

ORGANIZATIONAL STRUCTURE

Explorer post, or Venturing crew) is expected to attend, if only to pick up flyers and packets of Scouting information. Some of these will be information on council and/or district training opportunities and events that you can participate in.

Your district will assign a unit commissioner (a volunteer) to help you with any questions or problems you might have because, as stated above, your DE is responsible for *a lot* of troops, packs, and crews. These commissioners can quickly answer many of your questions because they have typically been active in Scouting in your area for quite a few years and simply know a lot. Ideally, your commissioner will come visit your unit, possibly as often as once a month, but the reality is that most don't visit nearly that often. If the District notices a problem with your unit, such as leaders who aren't fully trained, your unit commissioner may contact you to help resolve it.

Cub Scouts is for kids from age 5 to 11. Scouting BSA is for youth age 11 to 17 and is where they can become Eagle Scouts™. Venturing®, Explorers, and Sea Scouts are all technically part of the "Venturing" program for youth age 14 to 20 or who have finished 8th grade and have been co-ed for many years. As you might guess, Sea Scouts has activities on water as well as land. When they pass these ages, they are said to "age out" of that level.

3. Unit Organization

> "If you make listening and observation your occupation you will gain much more than you can by talk." (Lord Baden-Powell)

Here is a short answer to how a unit is organized. The Cubmaster/Scoutmaster is the creative side, the energetic showman. The Committee Chair is the administrative lead. The COR (Chartered Organization Representative) is responsible for ensuring everyone is doing their job well and for vetting new leaders. Volunteers who work directly with Scouts (such as den leaders and ASMs) report up to the Cubmaster/Scoutmaster. Volunteers who do not work as directly with Scouts (the treasurer and secretary) form a Committee that reports to the Committee Chair.

PACK ORGANIZATION

Adult Leadership

The Cubmaster/Scoutmaster, Committee Chair, and COR are the **Key Three** for the unit. Units absolutely may not have the same person in two, much less all three, of the Key Three positions. The Key Three concept is replicated at the District level all the way up through National. If any of these positions is vacant, the unit can't recharter (discussed in Chapter 8), which means it will be disbanded.

The Committee Chair is generally in charge of recruiting adults, rechartering, and most administrative tasks. The Committee always includes the treasurer, secretary, membership, and unit trainer. The rest of the Committee depends on your unit. Fundraising chair, quartermaster, and service chair are all common but a truly tiny unit may not need these, or even have enough adults to fill the roles. In Scouts BSA, the Committee is responsible for planning and conducting Boards of Review for rank advancement.

The Cubmaster/Scoutmaster oversees program–what the Scouts actually *do,* most especially the meetings–and the volunteers who work most directly with the Scouts, especially den leaders and ASMs. While the Cubmaster plans and runs pack meetings in their entirety, Scoutmasters role in troop meetings is generally limited to any announcements they have and a "Scoutmaster Minute" (discussed in Chapter 4). They are critical to youth advancement, however, because they are involved in the Merit Badge (MB) process and every rank except Scout includes a Scoutmaster Review, followed by a Board of Review.

Den leaders run den meetings. They normally plan the entire meeting, which is much easier if you use the resources made available by BSA and online. These resources include very detailed meeting plans.

ASMs (Assistant Scoutmasters) help the Scoutmaster with outings and other program-side activities. In Scouts BSA, most of the program is led by the youth so the joke is that adults spend campouts napping in their hammocks. Of course, adults are responsible for

PACK ORGANIZATION

safety and "boy led" doesn't mean "adult abandoned", but it is important to remember **your primary role is to guide, not to do**. If the Scoutmaster isn't available, if the youth is their child, or if the unit is very large, ASMs may also be asked to do Scoutmaster conferences. The larger the unit, the more likely it is that individual ASMs will be tasked with specific tasks such as overseeing individual patrols or activities.

Of course, how things work ideally and how they work in the real world are often two completely different things. If you enter the web address below, you will find a 16 page document explaining the intended/ideal "Cub Scout Pack Organization" in great detail, and with both requirements and responsibilities for all positions, on scoutingbsa.org. It's probably a bit much to take it all in while you're getting started, but it's good to go back and review later.

scoutingbsa.org/programs/CubScouts/Cub_Scout_Unit_Structure.pdf

It is important for unit leaders to be spread throughout all the levels, not clumped in one year group. This happens naturally for den leaders, but if a unit ends up where the Cubmaster/Scoutmaster, Committee Chair, Secretary, Activities Coordinator, and only adult with outdoor training (required for camping) are parents of kids who are about to age out with no younger children in the unit, what condition do you think the unit will be in the next year?

Some units have, or have had, one Scouter who is the Committee Chair, Cubmaster, COR (Chartered Organization Rep), den leader, chief cook, battle washer, and heads up two committees, in addition to holding down a full time job. Whew! What's the downside, beyond the fact that they clearly lied on their recharter? It's that many fewer people to recruit, right? Not so fast. What happens if that Scouter's son drops out or they move? How about when they age out? How will those who come after them know which tasks go with each separate job? Does anyone else know how to do *any* of their jobs? How well are they doing these jobs? How well could these jobs be done if

PACK ORGANIZATION

several people were each focused on doing one job and doing it well?

That's a lot of questions to ponder—and that's *a lot* of vacancies to fill at once when they eventually move on, which can lead to a lot of floundering. One person holding multiple positions also doesn't encourage different points of view on the Committee, and gives that person a great deal more influence than any other individual Scouter or parent, intentional or not. That is part of the reason that volunteer *committees* of adults support the unit. It isn't just one person making all the decisions.

YOUTH RANKS

Cub Scouts are organized into dens, which are smaller units of Scouts within Cub Scout packs and Scouts BSA are organized into patrols for the same reason. Dens/patrols are groups of normally four to six Scouts (but not more than ten or things get crazy) in the same rank within Scouts. Depending on its size, a pack may have one den or several for any given rank. For example, one year our pack had one den each of Tigers, Bears, and Wolves, two of Webelos 1s, and three of Webelos 2s. Troops have the choice of grouping youth into patrols so everyone the same age is together or so each patrol has youth of all different ages. Each year, those numbers change as new Scouts join in each grade, and others leave due to sports, changing interests, and family moves. One thing that is the same across Cub Scouts and Scouts BSA is that dens and patrols are always single-gender with separate ones for boys and girls.

New youth in Cub Scouts and Scouts BSA must earn a "joining" rank where they learn the basics about Scouts. For Cubs, this is their Bobcat, which is why it is in the beginning of all handbooks. The Bobcat is their introduction to Cub Scouting, whether they are five years old or ten years old. Lions is a new program for 5 year olds and they are the youngest Cub Scouts, followed by Tigers (6 year olds or 1st graders). Lions and Tigers are new to Scouting, and still little guys, so one of their parents must be with them at all activities, including

PACK ORGANIZATION

den meetings.

The next two levels are Wolf (7 year olds, 2nd graders) and Bear (8 year olds, 3rd graders). The final rank in Cub Scouts is Webelos (Webelos: We Be Loyal Scouts). These Scouts are 9/10 year olds or in 4th/5th grade. Webelos 1 (Web 1) and Webelos 2 (Web 2) are officially non-existent ranks, but they are widely used in common parlance. ("Web" is pronounced with a long "e", like "Weeb".) Generally, Web 1 means 4th graders and Web 2 means 5th graders. Because they are preparing to join Scouts BSA, Webelos are often given more independence and responsibility in the pack. They can also be referred to as Webelos (4th grade) and Arrow of Light (5th grade) dens because those are the ranks they focus on.

When they turn 11 or are ten and have earned their Arrow of Light, Webelos may cross over into Scouts BSA. Boy Scouts of America is the over-arching organization that encompasses all Scouts, including Cub Scouts, but when the term "Boy Scouts" is used within the organization, it generally refers specifically to the level Scouts enter when they cross over from Webelos. The official name for that is now "Scouts BSA" but the reality is that it will probably take years for Scouters to stop referring to it as Boy Scouts.

"Scout," the first rank for Scouts BSA, requires them to understand how a troop is supposed to function and to know the Promise and Law. Tenderfoot, Second Class, and First Class focus on Scout skills including camping, citizenship, fitness, navigation, first aid, emergency preparedness, and more. There is a pamphlet at the beginning of every Scout book (Cub and Scouting BSA) for parents to talk with their children about child abuse. This is usually the hardest requirement to finish for Scout rank, because parents have to confirm it's done. For Tenderfoot through First class, it's the fitness logs because Scouts forget to log their exercise.

In Scouts BSA, Scout through First Class can all be worked on simultaneously but the remaining ranks (Star, Life, Eagle) must be com-

PACK ORGANIZATION

pleted in order and one cannot be started until the one before it is completed. Through First Class, Scouts are learning Scouting skills and ideals, how to work as part of a unit, and skills to be self-sufficient, like cooking and navigation. Star through Eagle focuses on developing leadership skills and encourages Scouts to try new skills, possibly even leading to a profession or life-long hobby through merit badge explorations.

When it's all new, it can seem a bit confusing, but it really does sink in and make sense, eventually. Parents and leaders are there to look out for the Scouts and provide a safe space for them to grow and develop. Scouts get more challenges and responsibility every year.

YOUTH LEADERSHIP

Scouts BSA is youth-led, adult managed. Adults are primarily responsible for safety issues but they also manage finances and guide youth to ensure a solid program. The senior youth leader is the **Senior Patrol Leader (SPL)** and each patrol is led by a Patrol Leader. The most common thing for adults to tell youth in Scouts is "ask your SPL" followed by "ask your patrol leader" because youth really are supposed to go to other leaders for help. **The hardest thing about being an adult leader in Scouts BSA is figuring out the balance of how to appropriately balance helping/guiding/interacting with youth and making sure they are the ones leading.**

In larger units, the SPL is helped by one or more ASPLs, or Assistant Senior Patrol Leaders. If they have more than one, each will typically be assigned a program area they are responsible for such as new Scouts or outings. Patrol leaders will also normally have an assistant, particularly for times they are swamped with school work or when they can't make a meeting or outing.

If the SPL isn't at a meeting or outing, an "acting SPL" takes the lead. For summer camps and outings where you know in advance that the SPL won't be there, the acting SPL should be active in planning and preparation as well as leading the actual event.

PACK ORGANIZATION

Youth leadership mirrors at least some of the committee as well as having program-side leadership. Lists of all the positions (quartermaster, secretary, Chaplin, etc.) are widely available but the Scoutmaster can also add unit-specific positions. One possibility, and one I strongly encourage larger units to replicate, is a Medic. This Scout needs to be very solid on their basic First Aid skills and, at a minimum, needs to have their First Aid MB but preferably also be CPR certified. They are responsible for checking out injuries at meetings and on outings. They care for those they can and have adults care for those they can't. They are also responsible for ensuring troop first aid kids are fully stocked and medicines aren't out of date.

Your unit may come up with another fantastic position for youth.

4. Meetings, Meetings, Meetings

> "A WEEK OF CAMP LIFE IS WORTH SIX MONTHS OF THEORETICAL TEACHING IN THE MEETING ROOM." (LORD BADEN-POWELL)

District Committee Meetings. Roundtable. Pack Committee Meetings. Leader Meetings. Pack/Troop Meetings. Den/Patrol Meetings. So many meetings! What is the point of them all? How often are they? Which ones should you attend? This chapter starts with the highest level meetings that you are likely to hear about as a unit leader and continues down to the boy-focused den/patrol meetings.

You need to attend your unit meetings–committee and/or leader meetings, pack/troop meetings, den/patrol meetings–but others are more optional, especially if you aren't the Cubmaster/Scoutmaster or Committee Chair. Roundtable is the most important of the optional meetings. It really does benefit you to attend, whenever you can and no matter what your position, even if it isn't every month.

Leader Meetings

Monthly **District Committee Meetings** are the district version of a pack leaders meeting. As a Cub leader, you probably don't need to attend them but you may choose to go. The only time I went during my first two years as Cubmaster was to have our recharter packet checked. These may be held right before the district Roundtable.

Roundtable is a monthly meeting for leaders from all the units in a district. Each unit should send at least one leader, but sending two or three is even better. Attendees network, receive information from council, and discuss any concerns or problems they have. It sounds short and simple, but don't underestimate how much you can gain from both the more experienced Scouters (many Scoutmasters are former Cubmasters) and the district commissioner's program. Like training, attending Roundtable helps leaders earn knots (adult leadership awards).

Pack/Troop Committee Meetings and **Leader Meetings** are where the pack leadership gets together to plan and discusses any problems or potential problems. Committee Meetings are when the budget and pack calendar are reviewed, discussed and finalized, and are led by the Committee Chair. Leader meetings focus more on pack and den meeting activities, and are led by the Cubmaster.

Cubmaster/Scoutmaster Minute

At the end of pack and troop meetings, the Cubmaster/Scoutmaster has a minute to speak. These are intended as inspirational short stories or thoughts to motivate youth to reach for Scouting's ideals. Naturally, there are tons available online and they are normally tailored to either the season or current events, including upcoming outings. While some Scoutmasters take the opportunity to speak for several minutes, everyone appreciates brevity in speakers and this is no exception. Regularly including something from *Boy's Life* magazine, especially the comics, is a great way to inspire more youth to read it.

Annual Planning Meeting

For Cubs, this is adult-led but youth input is invaluable to making sure the kids are excited. For Scouts BSA, it is youth-led but adults are still there to supervise. Most units, no matter the level, have annual activities that are the first things plugged into the calendar. There are also district level activities, such as camporees and family campouts, that should be entered next. Your district should have an annual calendar available. Ask around if you don't have a copy.

This isn't the time to get into the weeds on what activities will be at every meeting. It is the time to figure out themes for every month, major outings youth want to do, and general goals for the unit. Those themes and goals will be the starting point for monthly PLC meetings when individual meetings and outings are planned in more detail.

The end of the school year/beginning of summer is a great time to do planning, especially for Cubs. For summer activities, it's best to give families the dates in the winter so they can plan around them. If you wait until April, they will probably already have their summer booked.

Youth Meetings

Pack/Troop Meetings, Den/Patrol Meetings and PLC (Patrol Leader's Council) are the meetings that include Scouts.

The PLC is specific to Scouts BSA and is where the youth leadership meets to plan and discuss any problems. They are normally held once per month so the youth can plan the meeting activities for the next month. The PLC normally has a planning meeting either once or twice a year to outline the schedule for the next year, which will be filled in during the monthly meetings.

Pack meetings include every Scout in the pack and can be some-

MEETINGS, MEETINGS, MEETINGS

thing boys dread, or their favorite part of Cub Scouts. It's up to the Cubmaster and their team. The more pack meetings **actively** involve the whole pack, the more likely the Scouts will love it. The more it becomes the Cubmaster Show focused on announcements, proclamations, and generally boring-sit-and-listen-quietly time, the less they will like it.

Troop meetings are when youth work on skills, do service projects, and generally prepare for outings and rank advancement. Most Scoutmasters do Scoutmaster conferences during meetings and most Committees do Boards of Review during meetings. Both of these are required for every rank from Tenderfoot through Eagle.

Most troops aim to have a campout/outing every month. Troop meetings for that month focus on skills related to that campout. For example, a January snow campout would lead to meetings focused on safe cold weather cooking and camping, as well as first aid for cold weather injuries. A canoeing trip would lead to a focus on water safety and first aid, and basic watercraft skills, and so on.

In addition to outing-related skills, troop meetings are when menus are planned and tasks are assigned. The SPL (or Acting SPL) should make tent assignments, following YPT rules, which are reviewed by the Scoutmaster or the ASM in charge of the outing. (Short version of YPT tenting rules: no Scouts alone in tents, no youth tented with someone more than two years younger than them, and obviously no boy/girl tenting.) The adults also review the menus and either approve them or ask for changes to make them healthier. Menus can be group-planned by the patrol or the Grubmaster (cook and shopper) can be responsible for menu planning, too.

Den meetings only include boys of the same rank. They can be at the same location as pack meetings, at a den leader's home, or somewhere else entirely, as long as Youth Protection Training (YPT, discussed in Chapter 6) is followed. Some den meetings, particularly for younger Scouts, are outings, hikes, projects, etc. that cannot be done

MEETINGS, MEETINGS, MEETINGS

at the regular meeting location. Den meetings are where most of the real work toward rank and other awards is done.

Patrol meetings are where youth in the same patrol get together to plan activities, work toward rank, or whatever else they need to work on. They can do many of the same activities as troop meetings, just with less youth involved. Patrols can definitely have their own campouts. It's a great way to help youth bond! As always, YPT rules apply. Patrol meetings, especially short ones, may be done within the troop meeting, before/after it, or at another time and place entirely.

5. Popcorn Sales and Fundraising

> "Scoutmasters need to enter into boys' ambitions." (Lord Baden-Powell)

The main fundraiser for Cub Scouts is the annual popcorn sale. It starts in August and continues through the fall. Motivated Scouts may continue to sell throughout the year by selling online. The Popcorn Kernel (not Colonel) is the volunteer who leads the unit (or District) popcorn fundraising efforts. The Kernel and your sale are usually very important to the financial health of your pack, and BSA needs the income as well.

There are other opportunities for fundraising. Scouting Magazine (the BSA magazine for Scouters) regularly has ads for some of them. You need to submit a simple application form for any additional fundrais-

POPCORN SALES AND FUNDRAISING

ers. (The page www.scouting.org/filestore/pdf/34427.pdf also contains official BSA guidelines for "money-earning projects".)

> <u>Important Note</u>: Packs and troops cannot solicit direct submissions of cash, including at popcorn booth sales and similar events. If people *offer*, your pack is certainly free to accept, but you may not *request or suggest* a cash donation.

It can be hard to get excited about selling $18 bags of popcorn, but it really is important to the financial health and well-being of BSA and your individual unit. Approximately 70% of the money stays with Boy Scouts, so each bag definitely makes a difference to BSA and your unit.

Selling popcorn is good for the boys too. The chance to earn money to pay their own way can be very empowering for them, and they learn a lot through the process. If you go to the link following this paragraph, it will explain the process and the benefits to boys quite thoroughly. Reading it is not essential for being a leader, but it does help. Honestly, it helped me a lot as a parent. It outlines the benefits for boys in truly committing and working to sell popcorn for the pack, which helped me be more genuinely enthusiastic about getting my son out to sell popcorn.

meritbadge.org/wiki/index.php/Popcorn

6. Training

> "Success in training the boy depends largely on the Scoutmaster's own personal example." (Lord Baden-Powell)

Youth Protection Training (YPT)

Youth Protection Training (YPT) is a key component of BSA's efforts to protect youth from abuse. There is nothing optional about it for leaders. Parents should be strongly encouraged to take YPT because leaders need to enforce YPT standards with everyone, not just those who have taken the training. Those standards include never having an adult alone with a child who is not their own. The easiest way to ensure that adults don't think you are "picking on them" when you enforce YPT is to have them take the training.

TRAINING

All adult leaders are required to take YPT, which is good for two years. It must be retaken every two years and does get periodic updates. YPT is available online at myscouting.scouting.org. The instructions below can be copied and sent to adult leaders.

If you haven't already, please go to myscouting.scouting.org and create an account. After logging in, click the graphic for Youth Protection Training in the right hand navigation. Youth Protection Training (YPT) is prominently featured. After finishing the course, ask people to print the certificate and bring it to whoever holds these for your pack at the next meeting. They can also select "view certificate" to download the certificate so they can email it to whoever needs it within your unit. Printing doesn't always work, and it may just be the wallet size that prints, but the important thing is to have proof you have taken it, just in case, because it is an absolute requirement at recharter.

OTHER ONLINE LEADER TRAINING

If you need other online training, including den leader and other position-specific training, it is available the same place.

In addition to YPT, everyone in the pack leadership, including Den Leaders from Tigers through Webelos, must take position-specific training, available at the same website. Each den level has a different leadership class for the den leaders. To be considered fully trained, committee members have their own training as well, naturally including YPT. There is additional supplemental online training that is not job specific, such as Safe Swimming and Weather Hazards. While no leader is required to have the supplemental classes to be considered fully trained, all leaders benefit from taking them and someone in the pack leadership should definitely take the classes because they are required for some outings.

UNIT TRAINER

Every unit should have a Trainer who follows up with each leader to ensure they are fully trained in a timely manner. The trainer should

TRAINING

maintain a folder or binder full of printed certificates proving what training each leader has taken. These are valuable backups if council loses their proof of training. First Aid (Red Cross) training can be done in a wide variety of places, so council may not have documentation for everyone who has Red Cross in your pack, so take particular care to ask for documentation for anyone who takes First Aid outside of Scouting. The Trainer is a good person for the Committee Chair to include on the Rechartering Committee (discussed below) because YPT is typically a key issue for rechartering.

Leaders with expiring YPT should retake it at least one month before their current YPT expires or before recharter is due, whichever comes first. When people take YPT, they need to either print their certificate and give it to the pack trainer or email them a copy of it, as discussed above. As new leaders sign up (Committee Members, den leaders, ASMs, or any other position), the trainer needs to make sure they do YPT *and* position-specific training with a goal of making sure the unit is and remains 100% trained.

The pack leader will receive a roster in the fall that includes all the Scouts® and Scouters, and lists when YPT expires for Scouters. Some leaders with expiring YPT will probably be parents who are about to leave the unit. Reminding them Web 2 parents, in particular, that their YPT is expiring is a nice courtesy because Scouts BSA troops require YPT as well.

ADDITIONAL TRAINING OPPORTUNITIES

In addition to online training, most councils and districts have a variety of training opportunities throughout the year, including large events such as Pow Wow and University of Scouting. Pow Wow is specifically for Cub Scout adults and University of Scouting is for all levels of Boy Scouting. They will also have smaller, more focused events that only offer one or two courses, such as BALOO (discussed below) or First Aid, and longer courses, such as Wood Badge.

Pow Wow and University of Scouting are the main training events in

TRAINING

most councils, as evidenced by the fact that they are specifically mentioned in requirements for more than a few knots. These events are for **all Scouters** not just the Key Three, or den leaders. Parents not in leadership positions are welcome to attend and learn more about Scouting as well. It is really difficult to oversell the importance and usefulness of Pow Wow, University of Scouting, and Roundtable.

You may be a bit overwhelmed by all the classes you can take at these two events. It may help if to decide in advance what you want to learn about (e.g., outdoor skills, leading den meetings, general skills like leading songs), or even ask the unit leaders to send you a list of which classes they suggest you take.

At my first Pow Wow, I focused on classes about awards with a few introductory classes on topics like Blue & Gold; another leader took BALOO; and the new Assistant Cubmaster focused on nuts and bolts classes and took an optional class on teaching the Whittling Chip. Having multiple people with different focuses let us cover a lot of ground in one day. My second year at Pow Wow, I focused on running pack meetings and Cubmaster-specific training.

> Important Note on Pocketknives: Make *VERY* sure knives are returned to adults after campouts or other use to help ensure Scouts never, ever accidentally take them to school. Of course, if you meet at a school you almost certainly cannot work with knives there.

Not only are these great places to get training, they are a great time to network and build ties within your own pack leadership. You really should take advantage of them. They will also help you advance toward leadership knots, some of which require attending these events. (These events may be combined in smaller councils.)

OUTDOOR SKILLS TRAINING

Some council and district events will offer BALOO–Basic Adult Leadership Outdoor Orientation. You MUST have at least one BA-

TRAINING

LOO trained adult—more is better, of course—at any outdoor event, most particularly camping. You must also have one person who has Red Cross™ First Aid with you when you go camping.

The BALOO and First Aid trained adults can be two different volunteers, or one person with both sets of training. Each pack must determine its own comfort level, keeping in mind that leaders are parents first. If their child is sick or injured, they may have to cancel at the last minute.

For Webelos camping, there is Outdoor Webelos Leader (OWL) training. The outdoor training for Boy Scouts is Introduction to Outdoor Leader Skills (IOLS), and I have been told it is 90% the same as OWL training. They can be offered together, meaning the trainee is still set when they move to Boy Scouts with their son. OWL training is a great addition, but you can go camping even if you don't have anyone with that training. The same cannot be said of BALOO, so it needs to be the first priority for outdoor training in every pack. IOLS is required for an ASM to be considered fully trained. OWL and IOLS training may be available at Scout summer camp and that is an extremely convenient option. I encourage you to take advantage, if you have the option.

Wilderness First Aid (WFA) is an advanced first aid class that takes approximately two full days, after you finish the CPR certification pre-requisite. It is required for a certain number of adults on high adventure trips with older youth to have this training but it's not bad for anyone. WFA is designed for when you are more than an hour from care such as a doctor or hospital. This can happen at the far point of a long hike or if you live in a particularly rural area, so it's something to keep in mind.

Last, but far from least, Wood Badge is an advanced training class for Scouters. Anyone who has earned the distinctive Wood Badge neckerchief and bolo tie with wooden beads is dedicated Scouter and a great source of Scout knowledge.

TRAINING

YOUTH TRAINING

ILST (Introduction to Leadership Skills Training) is the first leadership training offered to young Scouts. Typically, troops want everyone in the PLC (all the youth leaders) to have this training. Scouts are required to have this before continuing on to NYLT and, later, possibly even NAYLE.

ILST has three modules of 30-60 minutes each and can be taught within the troop. The three modules are troop organization, tools of the trade (communicating, planning, teaching), and leadership and teamwork. The troop goal should be to have this with a few weeks, at most, of starting a new term of office. If it will be more than that, the Scoutmaster will need to do a brief orientation for Scouts who are new to the PLC.

Many Scouts do not take the more advanced leadership training available to them such as NYLT and NAYLE. In recognition of those Scouts who do go the extra mile and take those classes, they earn special uniform neckerchiefs when they complete the course.

NYLT (National Youth Leadership Training) is a six day training course available to Scouts 13 or older and First Class or above, with the recommendation of their Scoutmaster. It can be taken as a full week or two three day weekends but no matter how or where it is taken, the same syllabus is used and the same material is taught.

It extends and deepens Scouts' knowledge of how to be a leader. They are expected to develop a mission for their unit and actively work to improve their own unit through their service and leadership, based on the methods they learned at NYLT.

NAYLE (National Advanced Youth Leadership Experience) expands on what youth learned in NYLT. It is offered to youth fourteen and up, with Scoutmaster recommendation, at all four high adventure bases (discussed in Chapter 10). The material varies slightly based on the environment where it is being taught.

TRAINING

As you can tell, BSA provides a lot of training opportunities in a variety of formats. Every leader can, and should, be well trained. Much, but not all, of what each leader learns is up left to their personal needs and preferences. Clearly, YPT and job specific training are required, but there are tons of opportunities beyond these bare basics for each leader to focus in on what they want to learn. Remember: youth aren't the only ones who should have fun! When you go to training, especially big events, at least part of your time should be spent doing things you love or have always wanted to try. Your enthusiasm will be contagious when you bring it back to your pack!

7. Uniforms

> "Show me a poorly uniformed troop and I'll show you a poorly uniformed leader." (Lord Baden-Powell)

In September 2013, BSA launched a website (BSAuniforms.org) specifically devoted to the uniform and how to wear it. There are pages devoted to Cubs, Webelos, Scouts BSA, and Leaders. This is a great resource to email new Scouts, leaders, and Webelos. The Webelos field uniform is different from the uniform for younger boys because they have the option of wearing the tan Boy Scout shirt. Even the blue uniform is slightly different because only they can wear Webelos colors.

A pack t-shirt is the most common activity uniform. This is unoffi-

UNIFORMS

cially also referred to as a "class B" uniform. It is worn for most den meetings and activities. Yellow and blue (the Cub Scout colors) are, not surprisingly, the most popular colors for Cub Scout pack Class Bs and each has its good and bad points. Scouts in dark blue shirts can seem to virtually disappear in the dark at campouts and other outdoor events, while yellow shirts are more visible. On the other hand, blue shirts hide more dirt and stains than yellow t-shirts.

All Cub Scouts from Tigers through Webelos can wear the all-blue uniform. Webelos have the option to switch to the tan and olive uniform of Scouts BSA. These are referred to as the field uniform, or unofficially as the class A uniform. Many families switch their Webelos to tan shirts when their son outgrows their blue shirt or when they have a younger son join Cub Scouts and they pass the blue shirt along to him. Adult leaders (Scouters) wear the tan class A uniform, essentially as described below. Certain insignia are required on the uniform immediately and others are added as they are earned. Cubs, Webelos, Scouts, and Leaders each have slightly different patch placement. Your unit will probably be very happy with you if you email the official links (www.scouting.org/filestore/pdf/34282.pdf, for example) to them. Few people seem to find patch placement information quickly or easily.

Uniform inspections are not required, but your pack should do them periodically, if not monthly. A January uniform inspection can help ensure everyone has the full field uniform before the Pinewood Derby, Blue & Gold, and other special events, for example. While this isn't written in the uniform inspection sheet, BSA has now officially stated that field uniform shirts are required to be tucked in.

The official uniform inspection sheets include the rank-specific neckerchief slide. These are often skipped, lost, or replaced. They quite simply slide off easily if the back side isn't pressed closed very tightly, and Scouts rarely notice when it happens, so be on the lookout for errant slides. Scouts may also make their own new neckerchief slides

UNIFORMS

at summer camp or as a den or pack meeting activity.

The basic required patches for BSA uniforms are the purple World Crest, pack number, and council patch. The American flag is pre-sewn onto the uniform shirt's right shoulder. Other common patches include Bobcat and rank (for Scouts) and position patches (Den Leader, Committee Member) on the left sleeve for Scouters. A BSA Scout/Scouter is not technically out of uniform without the pre-sewn flag patch, although they are clearly expected to wear it. They are, however, out of uniform if they wear any other flag in place of the Stars and Stripes. (Please see the endnote if you are interested in some nit-picky, you'll-never-really-need-this information.)

Your unit can make choices to tailor the uniform requirements based on your needs, but that probably will not conform to official BSA standards, as reflected on the inspection sheets. In our pack, more than a few of our families have significant financial constraints. As a result, we don't ask parents to spend $14 for rarely-worn rank-specific caps, and we definitely don't ask them to buy official uniform socks as Cubs.

Cub Uniforms

The blue uniform is a blue Cub Scout shirt, blue Cub Scout pants, blue Cub Scout belt, blue Cub Scout socks (orange for Tigers), rank neckerchief with slide, and rank cap. The tan uniform for Webelos is a tan BSA shirt, olive green BSA shorts or pants, blue Cub Scout belt, olive green BSA socks, navy blue loops or tabs, and Webelos neckerchief with slide, cap, and colors. Webelos colors are a ribbon pin that goes on the right shoulder and all the Webelos activity badges (pins) can, in theory, be pinned on this. Belt Loops fit on the Cub Scout belt, but not on the Boy Scout belt.

Rank (Tiger, Wolf, Bear, Webelos) specific uniform items for Scouts are their neckerchief, cap, and slide. Tigers also have different socks. Packs may choose to have a special, custom pack neckerchief instead of rank-specific ones, although that is typically more for Boy Scout troops. Neckerchief slides are one place Cubs and older youth alike show their individuality with many making their own at camp or on outings.

SCOUTS BSA AND SCOUTERS

The Scouts BSA uniform is the tan BSA shirt, olive green BSA shorts or pants, olive green BSA socks, unit neckerchief with slide, and olive green shoulder tabs (loops) with the olive green BSA baseball hat or the olive green campaign hat. If they get the nylon pants, the belt is built-in but if they buy the heavier cotton ones, they need to buy a separate BSA belt. Many youth wear other BSA hats such as ones from summer camp. Older Scouts will often wear specialty neckerchiefs they earned through training programs or when they earned their Eagle.

The adult uniform is essentially the same as the Scouts BSA youth uniform except most adults don't wear a neckerchief unless they have earned the special Wood Badge neckerchief. Non-Wood Badge adults who chose to wear a neckerchief may either wear their unit neckerchief (if they have one) or the BSA adult Scouter neckerchief.

LOOPS OR TABS

You may have noticed that anyone wearing a tan shirt (Scout or Scouter) has loops of fabric (shoulder tabs) on their epaulets. If they don't, they should. Gold means area, regional, or national. Employees at the Scout Shops® are considered employees of national, so they have gold tabs. Silver means council or district, including district level volunteers such as commissioners and, technically, Chartered Org Reps. Dark green is for Venturing. Orange is for Varsity Scouts®. Olive green (and sometimes the pre-2008 red) is for Boy Scouts. Navy blue is for Cub Scouts.

Sometimes you may see fancy loops or tabs. BSA creates special commemorative loops for special events such as Jamborees®. These are only supposed to be worn for six months before and after the event, and then put away as a keepsake. Just know that these are not something you can pick up a Scout Shop. All the leaders in your Cub Scouts and any Webelos wearing tan shirts should wear blue tabs. Scouts BSA youth and adults wear olive drab.

Uniform Boxes and Misc.

There is a red felt vest (brag vest) Scouts can wear with fun patches on them (Pinewood Derby®, popcorn sales, etc.). There is also a red fleece jacket Scouters often wear for much the same reason.

Most units eventually have a cache of hand-me-down uniforms parts that are doled out to Scouts in need. Eventually, your uniform box will probably include tabs from past leaders and Scouts (blue or olive), along with Class A shirts, t-shirts, caps, neckerchiefs, and neckerchief slides. This is a great way to reuse and be thrifty.

You can create your own uniform traditions, such as having each Scout write their name on their neckerchief with sharpie, then returning it at crossing over. Eventually, each neckerchief will be covered in the names of Scouts who passed through the pack. This also conserves resources and money by reusing the same ones for years. (Credit where it is due: the idea is from Pat Gould's book *Someone has to Tell the Stories*.)

Uniforms serve a purpose. They instill pride and a sense of belonging, or at least they should. If everyone in your unit looks totally different or wears their uniform differently (and therefore mostly not following the uniform guidelines), then that sense of pride and belonging won't be instilled. The small amount of extra time it takes to ensure a neat and well uniformed unit is time well spent.

8. Rechartering

> "WE DO NOT WANT TO MAKE SCOUT TRAINING TOO SOFT." (LORD BADEN-POWELL)

Rechartering is about making sure your unit roster (the names and information for all the Scouts and Scouters in your unit) is up to date and every adult has all the training they need. There are other elements, but those are the bulk of the work. Very few members of a unit leadership work on rechartering, an administrative effort led by the Committee Chair. If you are not part of the recharter committee, feel free to skip the rest of this chapter. What follows is a very brief overview of the process, just enough to provide an idea of what needs to be done. Your council and/or district should provide the necessary training to complete the process.

RECHARTERING

The Training Coordinator and Membership Chair are good additions to the recharter committee, led by the Committee Chair. The Training Coordinator is responsible for tracking YPT and position-specific training. The can encourage the leaders to complete it all two months before recharter is due, allowing time to follow up on loose ends without being rushed and stressed.

At some point in the fall, the unit leadership should get a roster from council. The unit Training Coordinator should check and ask leaders to retake YPT if it expires anytime up to one month after your recharter packet is due. The Membership Chair needs to check the roster for members (Scouts or Scouters) who left your unit for any reason, and for any who are not included. They will probably ask den leaders to check as well.

The actual "rechartering" part is this: there is a (one) document in your recharter packet that is the "charter" for your pack. Each unit has a "chartering organization" and you should know who yours is. Your unit Charter Organization Representative (COR) takes this "charter" to your charter organization. When a representative from them signs, that's their agreement to continue chartering the pack. Congratulations! The actual "recharter" part is done. Yes, that part really is that easy (in theory), but of course there is more than that to the "recharter" process, as you will learn in training.

After your recharter is done, you will be evaluated for the Journey to Excellence (JTE). Per Scouting.org, "Scouting's Journey to Excellence is the BSA's new council performance recognition program designed to encourage and reward success and measure the performance of our units, districts, and councils." What does that mean to your unit? In short, it's how council rates each unit's performance, and how national rates each council's performance. What do they measure?

- <u>Advancement</u>–How many youth finished their rank and advance to the next level?

RECHARTERING

- <u>Retention</u>–How many youth in your unit last year are still members?
- <u>Recruiting</u>–How many new members do you have?
- <u>Meeting</u>–Do your unit, dens/patrols, and unit leadership meet regularly throughout the year?
- <u>Training</u>–Do you have unit leadership in place and trained?
- <u>Activities</u>–Do you have variety, year-round including outdoor, summer, service, day/resident camp, fitness, and more?
- <u>Finances</u>–Does your unit have a budget and involve youth in creating it?

The address following this paragraph takes you to a JTE evaluation form. You will get the information to complete the JTE paperwork during the recharter process.

www.scouting.org/filestore/mission/JTE_Pack_Requirements.pdf

Rechartering, and JTE to a lesser extent, is a lot like balancing your checkbook. It can be time consuming and a pain in the posterior–the longer you let it go, the more painful it is–but it isn't really complicated. Recharter forces units to purge and update their membership lists and to fill vacant leadership positions. It also forces leaders who are not up to date on YPT to become up to date, and YPT is very important to BSA for keeping youth safe.

9. Ranks and Awards

> "A fisherman does not bait his hook with food he likes. He uses food the fish likes. So with boys." (Lord Baden-Powell)

Scouts should have fun. No, they *must* have fun! If they do not have fun, they will quit. For that matter, Scouters will quit too, if they aren't having any fun, just not as quickly as the kids. I'm a leader and I love Scouting, and I've come very close to quitting when it was pure drudgery or when the other adults were being too difficult. (This is another reason one Scouter should not fill multiple jobs within a pack.)

Ranks and advancement are important, and earning awards is great (who doesn't like bling?) but they aren't the real point. Learning,

Ranks and Awards

growing, and maturing are the real point, and Scouting can't help kids do those things if they don't stay in. So, while they should earn rank and awards, it won't matter much in the long run, or keep them in the program, if they aren't having fun while they do it.

Ranks

Youth progress through the Advancement Trail as they go through Cub Scouts. The first step for a Tiger Cub is to earn his Immediate Recognition. This shows he has learned the Cub Scout salute, sign, and motto, all of which are part of the Bobcat. Then he will continue on to finish earning his Bobcat, which is the first step for all other new Cubs who are older than Lions and Tigers. The **Bobcat** is the Scouts' introduction to Cub Scouting. To complete their Bobcat, Scouts must:

- Show the Cub Scout sign, salute, and handshake and tell what they mean;
- Learn and say the Cub Scout motto, the Cub Scout Promise, and the Law of the Pack and tell what they mean; and
- Show they understand and believe that it is important to be honest and trustworthy.

While no Scout is required to earn rank (**Lion, Tiger, Wolf, Bear, Webelos**), my experience is that most do earn their rank each year, or at least get close. (One of the Journey to Excellence items is how many Scouts in a unit earn their rank.) The final step on the Cub Scout Advancement Trail is the Arrow of Light, which can only be earned by Webelos and is earned after the Webelos rank, unless they start Cub Scouts as a 5th Grader. As soon as the year ends and Scouts are promoted or cross over from one rank to the next, they are no longer able to earn the previous rank(s).

Some requirements are fun, such as practicing safe bike riding, but most boys will find at least a few of the rank requirements to be less fun, if for no other reason than because different kids like different things. Unsurprisingly, each rank is a bit more challenging than the one before it because kids grow up as they advance through the program.

School activities can count toward rank requirements. Many packs are based at elementary schools, so this makes a lot of sense. All the Scouts in each grade do the same thing. Where we have requirements that they have legitimately met at school, this lets kids finish rank requirements somewhat more quickly. This in turn gives them an extra meeting or two to focus on *fun!* Fun and challenges are what keep them involved, not simply working toward rank.

For example, the Citizenship pin for Webelos has an activity where they write a report about a famous American. They already do this in school. Most art teachers will do most, if not all, of the Artist requirements at some point in the year. Most packs don't have anyone who will do a better job of that in a den meeting or at home, so why not count it?

Another benefit is that sometimes counting school activities gets a youth close to earning a pin they otherwise wouldn't attempt. This happened with my son and the Webelos Showman pin. He would never, ever, in a million billion years, have earned Showman without including school activities. There was no point trying. However, including 4th grade music class got him close. He had an incentive to try new things to earn it.

Our pack has found that Scouts with very involved parents are already doing some of what they covered in school at home, but other kids need that extra bit of help to finish rank/awards. So, using school to fulfill requirements has a threefold impact: (1) allow more time for fun/extra activities; (2) get kids close enough to try to finish a pin they might not otherwise attempt; and (3) help youth who are involved in Scouting, but who do not get as much support at home for the program.

RANKS AND AWARDS

AWARDS

There is an award to suit every interest. There are patriotic awards, outdoorsy awards, service awards, religious awards, family awards, and so many more. It really is worth taking some time to review what's available.

It is important, of course, that they genuinely earn their ranks and other awards, but kids need to stay excited about Scouting. When you attend training such as Pow Wow, you may be able to take a class to learn more about all the available awards (every event has different classes available). You can also look at them online. There are *lots* of awards available.

The websites listed at the end of this book have more information on Cub Scout awards. Non-official ones may be slightly out of date, but they are sometimes easier to use and some of the awards are done in conjunction with other organizations, such as the Red Cross. The link below is to the official BSA website and all the information there should be completely up to date.

Religious award resources are available through Pray Publishing. There is a *very* long list of faiths and denominations with awards available. Scouts typically earn them through their family and their House of Worship, not their unit, unless their charter organization is also a religious organization. The unit should recognize any Scout who earns one of these religious awards at a pack meeting or troop Court of Honor. Very few Scouts ever earn them, so it's really a big deal when they do.

Temporary Patches are worn on the right pocket. They have a loop to attach over a button on the pocket flap. Only one may be worn at a time and they include the Tiger Cub Instant Recognition Award, the Whittlin' Chip, and the Webelos Compass Points Emblem. Scouts often receive them at Scouting events such as summer camp and camporees, for Webelos and older youth.

RANKS AND AWARDS

Cub Scout Awards
www.scouting.org/scoutsource/CubScouts/Leaders/Awards.aspx

The following are a few more commonly referenced or seen awards.

The Arrow of Light (AoL) is the highest award in Cub Scouting. This and religious awards are the only awards earned in Cub Scouts that may be worn on a Scouts BSA or adult uniforms. A green and red knot designates a Scouter who earned the Arrow of Light as a Scout. AoL is designed to help Cubs become familiar with Scouts BSA and ease their transition.

It is _very_ important to make sure you know the deadline for your council for entering the Arrow of Light as completed. If it is not entered in time, it may not show up as being earned when Scouts cross over into Boy Scouts, and it still won't be there when they become adults in Scouting.

The Cub Scout Outdoor Activity Award can be earned by any Scout who attends summer camp, and it can be earned every year. The first year, a Scout gets a patch to sew onto his right pocket flap. After that, he gets a pin ("device") to add onto that patch. It is really fairly easy for any boy who is active in the pack to earn, if he goes to summer camp.

Whittlin' Chip is earned by Cubs who learned how to safely handle a pocket knife. They may only have a pocket knife on Scouting outings after they have earned this card, and they must bring the card with them to carry a pocket knife. If they behave in an unsafe manner, the Whittlin' Chip is a privilege that can be revoked, forcing them to re-earn it. There is no set, prescribed course for leaders to take before teaching the boys how to whittle, but there are requirements for earning the Whittlin' Chip. There may be a course available at a training event, but taking it is not required.

Scouts BSA Awards
Totin' Chip is for Scouts BSA youth who have shown they know

how to safely use not just a pocket knife but also an axe and a hatchet. As with Whittlin' Chip, they need to carry their card with them, a corner (or more) is cut off for unsafe behavior, and it can be lost and need to be re-earned. It is often earned at summer camp, especially in the "first year" program, but not always.

Eagle Award is, of course, the Big Mama Award of all youth awards. It's the best known, oldest, etc. It is the highest award in Scouts BSA. After they earn it, youth can earn "Palms" that indicate they have finished more merit badges and remained active with their troop.

10. Summer Camp and Outdoor Activities

"A boy is not a sitting-down animal." (Lord Baden-Powell)

Go and have fun! If it isn't (mostly) fun, especially for the Scouts, then your unit needs to re-examine what it is doing. In addition to council sites, many locations, including state and national parks, have great programs for Scouting.

In all unit activities, including camping and hiking, variety is important. Some county, state, and national parks include, or are near, historical sites. Others are centered around natural beauty or activities like fishing. Take advantage of the variety and spice up your camping program by going somewhere new and different.

SUMMER CAMP AND OUTDOOR ACTIVITIES

The second most important point, which I made before in the training section, is that every pack ***must*** have at least one person with outdoor training (BALOO for Cubs and IOLS for Scouts BSA) and one with Red Cross training along on all campouts, for the entire duration of the campout, although this isn't a requirement for summer camp because they have staff to meet these requirements. To be clear, you can have one person with both sets of training, or one person with outdoor training and a different person with Red Cross, but there must be someone who has been trained in each area, as well as a person with current Weather Hazards training.

A unit leader must also bring Parts A & B of the Annual Health and Medical Record for everyone (youth and adult), and the Activity Consent Form (permission slip) for every Scout in attendance at every campout.

www.scouting.org/scoutsource/HealthandSafety/ahmr.aspx
www.scouting.org/filestore/pdf/19-673.pdf

These forms are actually required for any event that is not at your normal meeting location, including summer day camp, and can be filled out by a parent. Events over 72 hours (summer resident camp and some advance youth leadership training) require completing Part C of the Medical Record as well. Part C is a physical form that must be completed by a doctor, and it must be less than a year old. You should review the full requirements for medical records on the web page listed above. An additional section must be completed for High Adventure camps.

Hiking and camping are part of earning rank, the Arrow of Light, and certain pins and badges. Simply put, any unit that doesn't camp is making it difficult for Scouts to earn rank and awards

While no one wants to "take the 'outing' out of Scouting", BSA is about the Scouts first and foremost, not the "outing." Yes, this does seem to contradict the last paragraph, but individual youth may have

SUMMER CAMP AND OUTDOOR ACTIVITIES

disabilities that require accommodation. BSA has guidelines for those situations because they are still kids, and "a boy [or girl] is not a sitting-down animal," even one confined to a wheelchair. Other kids may have parents who are not supportive, making it difficult or impossible to participate in outings.

As I mentioned above, my unit commissioner, district executive, and I crafted a plan to allow a temporarily wheelchair-bound Scout to earn his Arrow of Light. If a Scout is genuinely unable to complete a requirement because of a disability, something can be worked out. In the case of the badly injured Scout in our pack, Plan B was for him to "participate in a hike" by doing all the planning for it, and it would not have been just talking up a hike a local park had planned.

SUMMER CAMP

Units often go to the camp run by their council but they are not required to. If you have younger kids in your unit, odds are good that you will go to a nearby day camp. If you have to drive back and forth every day, an hour or two drive each way is probably too much, but that same drive may be just fine to get to resident camp, when you are not driving home every night. The ability to go farther obviously gives units more choices. Even younger Scouts can go to resident camp, although it is often shorter for them.

As Scouts get older, your options expand further. Some camps offer special Webelos weeks. In our council, the smaller "day" camp offers a short (long weekend, not full week) Webelos camp. The regular Boy Scout camp has areas that are devoted to Webelos camps for the entire summer. That is a week-long program chock-full of adventures for boys. Many camps have a single week devoted to Webelos as their Scouts BSA camp.

Most boys come back from Webelos Camp excited about moving on to Scouts BSA. However, camps may offer the same program every year. Repeating it could bore some of them, causing them to lose interest in attending summer camp in the future. If your Scouts return

SUMMER CAMP AND OUTDOOR ACTIVITIES

to the same Webelos camp for a second year (Web 1 and Web 2 years), check to see if the camp has a different second year program and sign them up for it.

Another option is to go to a different camp. Different BSA camps have different focuses. Some are on the water (lake, ocean, or bay). Others are in mountains or woods. They may even focus on STEM–Science Technology Engineering & Math–or another program area. Depending on which camp a Scout attends, he has different opportunities. Your local council camp may not even be the closest to you, but it will almost certainly offer a lower price for in-council Scouts. Explore your choices!

PACK CAMPING

Cub Scouts is structured so that families are involved, including on camping trips. Webelos camping trips (without as many parents) are an option if you have someone who has taken the training. (BALOO is good for all Cub Scout camping; OWLs is specifically for Webelos camping.) Your Cubs should be making some progress toward rank on these trips, but they simply *must* have fun. If they aren't, they won't keep coming back.

While structured activities are important, and BALOO training discusses the structure for a campout, as Lord Baden-Powell noted, "Where is there a boy to whom the call of the wild and the open road does not appeal?" Let the kids enjoy the wild! In addition to structured activities, or as part of them, make sure they have time to run around, look at critters, explore a bit, and generally be kids. Of course adults will be supervising them, and hopefully they will be learning, but they don't need to know that.

On one campout, the Scouts did supervised activities including a scavenger hunt, nature walk, flashlight tag, and preparing dinner. For other activities, the adults stayed in the background and let them lead the way. As soon as they had a chance, they ran off to play in the woods. I saw one young man teaching the others how to skip rocks in the creek. If all their time had been structured, he would have lost that chance to take a leadership role, as would the Scout who chose to round up the others when they headed out a bit too far. The other kids would have missed learning how to skip rocks.

The first two campouts I went on had no set activities at all. That did not lead to the best experience for anyone, Scouts or parents. Plan activities in advance, but be flexible and prepared to change things as you go. The simple nature hike turned into the Scavenger Hunt mentioned above because the camp office had a Scavenger Hunt sitting there when we checked in so we ran with it. The youth loved it!

TROOP CAMPING

Pack camping is family camping. Troop camping is not.

Pack campouts are largely planned by adults. Troop campouts are planned by youth. The youth must make and carry out the camp plan, including creating a menu and a shopping list, buying things, cooking, and cleaning up, in order to earn their ranks and advance in Scouts BSA. This can be difficult for adults to get used to.

The primary responsibility of adults in Scouting BSA is safety. This really comes into play in camping. If it's August and youth are planning to have milk and eggs for breakfast after the second night of camping, you might want to direct them to make a different choice unless someone has a way to keep that food safe for two days.

For most established troops, the goal is to camp every month. While fancy trips like staying on a historical ship are great every now and then, the focus needs to be on basic Scout skills. That's what they joined for, not mini-vacations. If you have a new or small unit, you may have to settle for a camping trip every two or even three months.

Camporees are a great way to get your unit camping, see other troops, and have some fun. These are normally district or council events. A large number of troops get together to camp for a weekend and do activities based around a theme. Possible themes include Troutoree (fishing), zombie survival (emergency preparedness), STEM, and Scouting skills. There was a Scottish Games themed one that focused on Scouting skills and another that somehow involved a famous sci-fi movie.

Hiking

Our unit went to a local state park for a "Full Moon Hike" which helped Scouts work toward rank, the hiking award, and the astronomy award all at once! On another occasion, we did an Owl Discovery hike. The youth got to dig into sanitized owl pellets, touch stuffed owls, and see owls in their natural (nocturnal) setting. More importantly, both events got the kids excited by being *different*.

In addition to doing different hikes and campouts in the spring and fall, you will probably want to change them from year to year. To keep it fresh, one experienced Scouter told me they rotate camping and hiking activities on a three year schedule. If you do the same hike, no matter how cool, every spring and every fall, it will quickly lose any appeal.

It really is difficult to imagine Scouting without summer camp, unit camping, and hikes. They have always been and will always be an integral part of Scouting. In my opinion, it is more important to leave plenty of time to explore when kids outside than in any other program area. Kids will find their fun. Whether it's climbing the perfect climbing tree, skipping stones, looking for owl pellets, or examining animal tracks, you simply cannot know in advance what absorbing mysteries and adventures your Scouts will find in the woods. So go with it! Adapt your plans as many times as you need to and embrace the fact that you have a group of kids enjoying the outdoors, with no electronics in sight.

Summer Camp and Outdoor Activities

High Adventure Bases

BSA has four main high adventure bases. "High adventure" activities are harder than young Scouts can manage, and riskier as well. They can involve being in places that only special satellite phones can reach for a week or more at a time. That is why it is critical to have people with current Wilderness First Aid training on these activities, and why it is even more critical to pay attention to physical requirements such as not being overweight or having other problematic health problems.

- Philmont: Based in New Mexico, the focus is back-country hiking, rock-climbing, and mule treks.

- Northern Tier: Based in the Minnesota, canoeing, kaying, portaging, and generally transporting oneself through the boundary waters with Canada is the focus, along with winter camping.

- Sea Base: Based in Florida and the US Virgin Islands, sailing, snorkeling, kayaking, fishing and scuba diving are the focus.

- The Summit Bechtel Reserve: The newest high adventure base in West Virginia has myriad activities including mountain biking, whitewater rafting, hiking, a skate park, zip-lining, and much, much more. It is also BSA's permanent location for national Jamborees. (Jamborees are big Scout gatherings.)

Scouts can typically go to high adventure bases when they are fourteen. They do have certain physical standards that must be met for youth and leaders, especially Philmont, for safety reasons. These are very guided trips, not loosey-goosey things where you can pop out to the store for forgotten items.

While it may seem like sailing in the Virgin Islands for a week couldn't possibly be hazardous, scuba diving is a high risk activity. One youth I personally know received a very deep cut from coral and

SUMMER CAMP AND OUTDOOR ACTIVITIES

then was stung by fifty (50!) sea urchins. Sunburn can also be pretty horrific for anyone who neglects their sunscreen.

Units typically enter a lottery 18-24 months before their intended trip and BSA lets them know if they were selected and, if so, how many "crews" they can bring. They will specify the number of youth and adults per crew. They also strongly recommend doing multiple shakedowns with all the youth and adults who are going to make sure your unit is ready. And by "they" in the last sentence, I mean not just BSA but pretty much anyone who has ever gone on a high adventure trip.

Many councils also have high adventure programs and there are similar programs run by outside organizations. Lenhonksin in Virginia, Swamp Base in Louisiana, Maine High Adventure, Tahosa in Colorado, Denali in Alaska…. The choices can be overwhelming, and that's without even looking at options in Europe. Depending on where your unit is, that can actually be a more cost-effective choice.

11. Special Events for Cubs

> "An invaluable step in character training is to put responsibility on the individual." (Lord Baden-Powell)

The Cubmaster plans and runs the pack meetings, but there are a few extra-special annual events that are planned and run by small committees that report back to the pack Committee. These events can be held during regular pack meetings, on a weekend, or any other time. They do not need to be at the normal pack meeting location but it's OK if they are.

Blue and Gold, Crossing Over, Arrow of Light

Units hold a **Blue and Gold dinner** every February, more or less, to celebrate the anniversary of the founding of Boy Scouts of America.

SPECIAL EVENTS

It is a birthday party for BSA, but not every unit celebrates on the same date. Awards are often presented at these dinners and a crossing over ceremony may be held as well. Usually, Scouts perform skits, sing songs, and otherwise provide entertainment for their families, and everyone enjoys a meal together.

Crossing Over is when Scouts officially transition from Cub Scouts to Scouts BSA. It is a special ceremony and needs to be treated that way. Some ten year old Scouts have spent five years–half their lives–working toward this goal. It is a really big deal for them. Scouts usually literally cross over a small bridge, walking from the Cub Scouts pack on one side to their new Scouts BSA troop on the other.

Packs may also choose to do a small "crossing over" at the end of the year for Scouts transitioning from one rank to the next one, but this is not an official crossing over. The only official "crossing over" is from Cub into Boy Scouts.

The Arrow of Light Ceremony may be combined with the Crossing Over Ceremony. There are *many* versions of each ceremony available online. As with Crossing Over, some of the youth have spent half their life working toward this goal and almost all will have worked very hard over the previous two years to earn it.

THE DERBIES

The Pinewood Derby is the reason my son joined Cub Scouts, and he isn't the only kid drawn into Scouts by it. The car-based Pinewood is the classic Cub Scout Derby, but there are also the Raingutter Regatta (for boats), the Space Derby (for rockets), and the Cubmobile Derby. The car in the Cubmobile Derby is actually large enough to hold a real, live child as it races. Some packs participate in all of these races so their pack has one each season, but that is entirely optional.

At its heart, the Derbies are about Scouts and their dad (or other adult) working together to turn some basic materials (like a block of wood and four wheels w/axles) into a lean, mean speed machine. Or

SPECIAL EVENTS

something like that. As always in Cub Scouts, the main point is to have fun while learning, growing, and staying safe.

For the Pinewood, generally the biggest derby, pack derby winners are invited to compete in district derbies, if the district has one. Cars are impounded after the tech inspection to ensure car construction followed the rules, just like at pack derbies, so tech inspection and the derby will probably be the same day. If your pack participates in a district derby, make sure the pack uses the same car building rules as the district. Our pack ended up with unfortunate circumstance of the winning car not being eligible for the district derby because we used different rules.

Not to harp on a theme, but these events are about having fun, and showing off a bit! When someone admires how cool the Wiimote Pinewood Car looks, the speed on a rocket, or the paint of a Cub-mobile, boys know they really did that. When everyone laughs at a great skit or claps for a fun song, they know it was really for them. That's tough to beat.

12. Service

"The Good Turn will educate the boy out of the groove of selfishness." (Lord Baden-Powell)

Do it. No ifs, ands, buts, or excuses. Service, like patriotism and faith, is an integral part of Scouting. If they are never *asked* to do for others, how do you think children will *learn* to do for others?

Service comes in many forms and doesn't need to be huge and time consuming. Our unit planted trees, spread mulch, and did landscaping. We collected DVDs and video games for a children's hospital, built cat scratchers for an animal shelter, and made felt story boards for the kindergarten and autism classes. Service can be a big project like older Scouts helping restore a building, or a small project like

SERVICE

weeding around your meeting place. Ideally, your pack will do a variety of projects–large and small, indoor and outdoor–so your Scouts learn that there are many ways to serve.

Scouting for Food is an effort by over three million Scouts nationwide to collect food for the hungry, generally in early November. Each pack receives plastic bags at a designated location such as a Roundtable meeting, which each Scout will distribute to homes in their neighborhood or another assigned area. Councils provide the date for the Saturday morning to drop off the bags. Scouts pick them up the following Saturday morning.

Donors should leave filled bags somewhere easily visible outside their home, such as near a mailbox or a back door, so Scouts don't need to disturb the homeowners when they collect donations. The food goes to a local pantry where it can help your community. Your district will probably have a central donation spot, but you may choose to donate to a different food pantry.

Every unit should definitely do a least one service project per year that supports their charter organization. If another organization provides meeting space, do something for them as well. In the past, our pack helped staff the annual fun run at the school and assisted with an outdoor classroom project.

Cubs, especially Webelos, can help decide which projects to do. In Scouts BSA, the youth should be the ones driving service projects, although the charter organization will probably have some specific requests. The youth will probably come up with some great ideas the adults would never have thought of. Webelos, in particular, also need to do a conservation project to earn their Arrow of Light. Local Boy Scout troops and county park services are good sources for conservation projects. Eagle projects are often conservation-focused and require a lot of volunteers.

Units that complete the **Messengers of Peace** program earn a ring

SERVICE

to put around the purple World Scouting Crest on their uniform. If you hadn't noticed, I'm a big fan of "bling." I think it helps motivate Scouts and lets them show off what they accomplish. Messengers of Peace is an incredibly easy to complete program. It is worth having someone make sure one of your service projects (you do more than one, right?) helps your Scouts earn the award so they can wear the patch.

Per Scouting.org, the Boy Scout program for young people is designed to build character, train them in the responsibilities of citizenship, and develop personal fitness. Service is an integral part of Scouting, not an optional add-on. It is important enough that service is part of how your unit's success is measured for the Journey to Excellence.

Even more importantly than all those official reasons, take the time to do a variety of meaningful service projects of all sizes so your Scouts, and possibly even the rest of their families, get in the habit of performing service.

13. Webelos and Transitioning from Cub Scouts to Scouts BSA

> "When you want a thing done, 'don't do it yourself' is a good motto for Scoutmasters." (Lord Baden-Powell)

In Cub Scouts, adults lead. In Scouts BSA, the youth lead. In Venturing, adults do even less. The older the Scouts are, the more responsibility they have. This can be a big change for parents. Instead of planning and leading the meetings, **parents are usually not even in the building during Scouts BSA meetings.** After being very involved in Cub Scouts, this can be quite an adjustment.

Losing Interest
It is not unusual for Web 2/Arrow of Light youth to lose interest in

SERVICE

Cub Scouts. Most have finished, or nearly finished, their Arrow of Light, are actively visiting Scout BSA troops, and may have gone to summer Scout Camp. They're ready to move on! But they have to wait until spring or even summer, depending on your council. How do you handle this? It's a struggle that packs and parents need to address in their own way, but the short answer is to **give them more responsibility, and possibly more privileges, within the pack**. They also need to know that it is expected, and required, for them to remain and be positive role models for younger kids.

Meeting Scout troops and doing activities with them is a great way to spark more enthusiasm. They need to see that Scouts BSA has activities to suit their interests and how much responsibility kids get within their own unit. There may be Patrol Leaders just a few months older than them. There will definitely be an older boy or girl they can look up to as SPL.

Transitioning

A well-done Webelos transition program helps ensure both parents and kids understand the coming changes. Ideally, one Webelos parent coordinates meeting as many local troops as possible, attending Camporees, and doing other activities preparatory to joining Scouts BSA. Different troops often have different focuses, based on the interests of Scouts (and Scouters) in those troops. Troops could be particularly interested in regular camping, backwoods camping, hiking, robotics, watercraft activities, high adventure, and many other areas.

Scouts really do need to actually meet the troops (plural–multiple troops, if available) to find the best fit for them, not just where their buddies want to go, the troop Cubs "always" go to, or the one closest to their house or their buddy's house. Youth should be strongly encouraged to go to both an activity and a meeting with a troop before signing up with them, if at all possible.

Scouts BSA

The never-ending, always see-sawing problem of Scouts BSA is how

SERVICE

to balance boy-led with adult-managed. It should never feel like the youth have been abandoned or like they have to do everything any adult says. The youth must lead. That's the entire point of Scouts. **Having a Scouts BSA unit where the youth aren't leading is like having a school where nothing is taught.** It entirely, utterly, and completely defeats the purpose. But they are still kids. Even at 17½, most have very little life experience. They need adult guidance and assistance, and they need to receive it from a variety of adults.

Finding the balance is always a challenge. Just when the leaders work out a good balance, the PLC changes, they have a new SPL, and things need tweaked. Maybe that's an overstatement but there will be times when it seems like the stone, cold, truth. Be prepared to change your approach. And be prepared to take a step back, or two, or three, then just to go sit in a camp chair or hammock and watch quietly while the Scouts handle everything. If you are doing regular Scoutmaster conferences with all the youth, any problems should come to light fairly quickly, while they are still fixable.

14. Assorted Scouts BSA Specific

> "It is risky to order a boy *NOT* to do something; it immediately opens to him the adventure of doing it."
> (Lord Baden-Powell)

The following information is from BoyScoutTrail.com. It is one of my favorite unofficial sites for Scout information. I highly recommend bookmarking it and spending some time perusing later. It has a looooooong list of useful information, including requirements. As with all unofficial websites, there is a risk of out of date information, so please confirm requirements with official BSA materials, but it is a convenient way to look up information quickly.

Boy Scout ranks and the focus for them are:

Scout–basic Scout knowledge

USEFUL WEBSITES AND APPS

<u>Tenderfoot</u>™–safety
<u>Second Class</u>–camping
<u>First Class</u>–self-sufficiency
<u>Star</u>–service
<u>Life</u>–leadership
<u>Eagle</u>–ultimate Scouting

Merit Badges

Merit badges are one of the first things most people associate with Scouts. There are over 130 of them and BSA updates them regularly by adding and deleting MBs, and by changing requirements. Realistically, no unit has MB counselors for every single MB. Most do, however, try to have at least one counselor for every Eagle-required MB.

MB Counselor is considered a district position so applications are given to district and your unit doesn't include them in recharter. This is a great place to get parents involved because the basic idea behind merit badges is to share something you love and/or know a lot about with kids who are interested in it. If they are nervous about how much time it might take, they can start with just one badge and add more later. Of course it requires YPT and this is a good way to get more parents to have YPT, something they need to drive youth on outings.

Scoutmaster Conferences

Every rank includes a Scoutmaster Conference. This is typically the last step before a Board of Review but it's OK to do it when there are one or two items left to be signed off, if that works out best for scheduling reasons and you are confident the youth will finish soon. **A good guideline is to have a Scoutmaster Conference with every youth *at least* every six months**, keeping in mind that ASMs can conduct Scoutmaster Conferences, too. They are a good way to touch base and see how youth are doing and what their goals are.

If a Scout has a goal of reaching Eagle but have been stuck, you may be able to find out the problem and help them move forward. It isn't unusual for youth to be absolutely, 100% positive that they haven't finished something when the adults can see they have. As kids, they just see the world a different way and many won't even ask because they are so sure it isn't done. The requirement to "select a campsite for your patrol and recommend it to your patrol leader" is a common source of this problem. Many campsites are predetermined locations with very few choices in where to camp and set up tents. In the minds of many youth, this means that they didn't finish the requirement. Adults view the requirement more leniently.

Once a Scout reaches First Class and is working toward Star, Life, and Eagle, it naturally takes longer to earn rank. Older youth are also busier with school, sports, jobs, and the rest of their life so they may not be as active, or progress as quickly, as they once did. You will also find that there are kids who just don't care about rank. They may have done literally every single item they need to do to earn Eagle but have refused to bring their book in to get sign offs for even Scout rank, and that's OK. Frustrating to the adults, but OK as long as the Scout is happy and having fun. For those kids who just don't care about rank, non-rank Conferences are still a good way to find out how they are doing and what they think the troop is doing well and could do better.

Scoutmaster Conferences are your chance to talk with youth to see how they are doing, how you are doing (are they happy?), how the unit is doing (what do they want to do more/less of?), and to be sure they are really learning. Please note that says "talk with" not interrogate, question, or talk at. It is a good time to be sure they are learning, but that doesn't mean it's time to review what they learned. That needs to be done as each item is signed off. If it's signed off, they have already demonstrated proficiency. There are lots of things for them to learn beyond rank requirements. If they aren't learning and growing, especially if you have a lot of youth who aren't learning and growing, that shows you an area for improvement.

BOARDS OF REVIEW

The final step in earning every rank except Scout is a Board of Review. Boards of Review are conducted by the Committee and generally take about twenty minutes. The main things to keep in mind are that you need three adults and that **no one on the Board can be an ASM or the Scoutmaster *for that unit.*** They may be in those positions in another unit. Boards of review are not a cross-examination or an attempt to confirm youth have learned whatever that rank required them to learn. That is presumed to have already been done.

One of the main goals for Boards of Review is to ensure youth are comfortable talking to adults and answering their questions. After several years of Scoutmaster Conferences and Boards of Review, job and college interviews should be much easier for them. It is common to ask them about their Scouting experience, school, and life in general. Let them talk, they will almost certainly surprise you, but prepare some questions to guide the discussion.

THE EAGLE PROCESS

The Eagle process is somewhat separate from the rest of advancement. There are significantly more checks to confirm youth have finished every single requirement correctly and in order. They should have a special person assigned to them by the District or Council who will help them through the process. The Scoutmaster Conference and Board of Review are also a bit different and involve people not otherwise involved in unit advancement. When you get to the point of having youth in the Eagle process, reach out to leaders in your area for more detailed advice.

ORDER OF THE ARROW

The **Order of the Arrow®** (OA) is the National Honor Society for BSA. OA develops leadership, a spirit of service, and an awareness of our environmental responsibilities in young men through a program that includes outdoor adventures, cheerful service, and celebrating American Indian culture.

USEFUL WEBSITES AND APPS

Members of OA of all ages, including adults, wear a special OA sash that is white with a red Arrow embroidered on it. OA members wear a lodge patch on their right pocket flap. Just as once you earn your Eagle you are always an Eagle, once you are a member of OA, you are always a member of OA, even if you become inactive.

15. Useful Websites and Apps

"In Scouting, a boy is encouraged to educate himself instead of being instructed." (Lord Baden-Powell)

Is there a specific program area where you need program help? There's an app and a website for that, possibly several. Scouting Magazine created a list of great apps, many sent in by experienced Scouters. Go ahead and use them! Apps to teach knots are also very popular. Your favorites will depend on your needs. It's an excuse to go shopping for new apps, many of them free! Woo hoo!

BSA is working on integrating technology into the program at all levels, including blogs, webcasts, and more. Have a great time looking at all these resources and remember to share the websites and apps with the leaders *and parents* in your unit! Specific links can be really helpful,

USEFUL WEBSITES AND APPS

and there are tools for parents and leaders at all levels, not just unit leaders.

Finally, because I couldn't think of where else to put this, **"YiS"** is short for "Yours In Scouting" and can be used in place of "Sincerely" in letters, emails, and other written materials.

Scouting Magazine's Ultimate List of Scouting Apps:

blog.scoutingmagazine.org/2012/08/09/the-ultimate-list-of-scouting-apps/

Official Boy Scout Websites

There are many great websites out there to help you in your Scouting adventures. BSA does try to keep up with the times while still respecting and holding to its traditions. As such, it now uses a blog, Twitter, multiple Facebook pages, podcasts, and all the other modern forms of communication. They've even created a reality TV show– "Are You Tougher than a Boy Scout?" Personally, I get a lot of information from the Scouting Magazine and Bryan on Scouting FB pages. The new Cubcasts are great too, and you can listen to them while commuting. Whatever format you prefer to get information in, BSA aims to provide it. Take advantage! That's what it's there for.

Be A Scout is the primary official online tool for recruiting. Scouting.org is the primary website for BSA, and Cub Scouts is a new website started in August 2013. As such, they have giant, enormous mountains of useful information and amazing materials for you. In my experience, this can be overwhelming. Take in small amounts at a time and don't try to jump in and read everything there at once. At the same time, it would be a shame not to use the resources that are right there at your mouse when you are ready. When you use the official sources, you can feel confident the information is correct.

Be a Scout–www.beascout.org

Boys Life Magazine–boyslife.org

USEFUL WEBSITES AND APPS

Bryan on Scouting (official BSA Blog for adult leaders)–blog.scoutingmagazine.org

BSA Uniforms–www.BSAuniforms.org

Cub Scouts–cubscouts.org

Scoutbook– www.scoutbook.com

Scouting.org–www.scouting.org

Scouting Magazine–scoutingmagazine.org

Your council website (a simple search should find it quickly)

Official BSA Facebook pages include: Boy Scouts of America, Cub Scouts, Scouting Magazine, and Are You Tougher than a Boy Scout?

Official BSA Twitter Feed–www.twitter.com/boyscouts

Cubcast/Scoutcast–www.scouting.org/ScoutCast.aspx

UNOFFICIAL SCOUTING-RELATED WEBSITES

These are a few sites I find useful. As with the official BSA websites, some have overwhelming amounts of information for all levels of Scouters. As we all know, unofficial sources are more likely to have outdated information and/or mistakes than the official ones, but these are generally well known and reputable sites. There are *many* more sites out there, many of them great. This list was selected with the goals of keeping it short, providing variety, and introducing some great, well-rounded resources to new Scouters, like you.

Boy Scout Trail–www.boyscouttrail.com

Lord Baden Powell quotes
– thinkexist.com/quotes/sir_robert_baden-powell

MeritBadge.org–meritbadge.org/wiki/index.php/Main_Page

USEFUL WEBSITES AND APPS

PRAY Publishing–www.praypub.org

Scout Insignia–www.scoutinsignia.com/index.htm
(part of the US Scouting Service Project's family of sites)

Scouter Mom–scoutermom.com

Scoutlander–scoutlander.com

Scouts Own–scoutsownplanningguide.faithweb.com

Scout Track–www.scouttrack.com

US Scout Service Project–www.usscouts.org

16. Final Thoughts

Even before BSA released updated training in 2018 that included associating with adults as one of the "aims and methods of Boy Scouting", I was a strong believer in the importance of youth finding a mentor there. In addition, having the chance to talk to adults who aren't family or teachers can help them with their first jobs and on through life, not just in interviews. (Getting youth comfortable in interview situations is an aim of Boards of Review.)

Scouters (and Merit Badge counselors) who share an interest with youth are in a great position to encourage them to expand that interest and to find new outlets for it, possibly even ways it can help them in their school, work, and personal life.

As a Scouter, you are a de facto role model. The youth see what you and the other adults in the unit do. Please be a good one.

Endnote

"The Scoutmaster teaches boys to play the game by doing so himself." (Lord Baden-Powell)

BSA uniforms come with the American flag pre-sewn onto the shoulder, so BSA clearly expects members to wear the flag. The following statement, which is directly copied from an email from National, clearly states it is not technically *required*, although it is expected.

In 1995, the BSA's National Executive Board finally addressed the flag problem by producing a statement which was published in SCOUTING magazine in the early part of 96 but has not been reprinted since: **"The wearing of the U.S. flag emblem is OPTIONAL on the part of our Cub Scouts, Boy Scouts, Explorers, and adult volunteers. Local Councils are not to mandate wearing of the emblem; however the Supply Division will continue** to provide uniform shirts with the emblem pre-sewn as a matter of courtesy for the wearer. If the Scout, Explorer or adult chooses not to wear the flag emblem, (my emphasis) *no other flag emblem, insignia, nor device* (end my emphasis) will be worn in that position in its place. If worn, only the U.S. flag emblem authorized by the Supply Division will be worn. Some members wearing the field uniform of the BSA are not American citizens; and certain religious faiths and observances may prevent some members from wearing the emblem of the United States of America.

To summarize what National wrote, individuals who have religious objections or who are not US citizens may choose not to wear the US flag on their uniform, but they may not wear another flag in its place. Also, if the pre-sewn flag is removed, it must be replaced by the same US flag emblem authorized by BSA Supply.

It is incredibly rare to encounter a Scout who refuses to wear the flag. You probably never will, but I choose to include this (incredibly hard to find) information just in case it helps some unit or leader.

About the Author

Bethanne Kim is a life-long Scout. She joined Girl Scouts in 1st grade and became a lifetime member at 21. Naturally, she only had boys, leading to her not-inconsiderable involvement in Boy Scouts.

Kim cares enough about Scouting that she not only agreed to be a Girl Scout troop Leader for girls in a county run half-way house, but to be an Assistant Leader for a troop locked up in juvi. They counted the pencils when the leaders entered and left, no pens allowed in jail, and the meeting area was surrounded by the girls' cells.

Her long list of Girl Scout accomplishments in, including earning the Gold Award, are one reason she was called on to become involved in Boy Scouts. She was a Cubmaster for four years, Assistant Cubmaster for two, and is currently an Assistant Scoutmaster and active member of the District leadership. Kim now has her PhD in Cub Scouting from Scout University and has taken enough classes in Boy Scouting to be a PhD Candidate in that, and it taking Wood Badge. She has been the ASM for New Scouts in a boy-led troop of over 80 boys, including over twenty new Scout, and is now the ASM for a brand new unit of nine that had two boys when she signed on.

Outside of Scouts, Kim earned her Bachelor's degree in International Studies from Johns Hopkins University, and is the happily married mom of two. She keeps busy building a website for dads (WiseFathers.com), blogging at TheModerateMom.com, and writing and promoting books.

Please take a minute to look at all her other books and to review this one on Amazon.

Other Books

Cubmastering: Getting Started as Cubmaster is an introduction for new Cubmasters. Topics covered include organizational structure, training, recruiting, and recharter. This is about more than just the nuts and bolts of Scouting, though. It also covers dealing with difficult parents and planning special pack events.

Citizenship in the World: Teaching the Merit Badge is, quite simply, a guide to assist merit badge counselors in teaching the BSA Eagle-required merit badge "Citizenship in the World." It includes the merit badge requirements, and information and tips for teaching it.

The Constitution: It's the OS for the US explains the historical context for the US Constitution and describes how it works using computer terms like firewall and plug-ins, not legalese. (An OS is a computer Operating System, like iOS for Apple devices.)

Survival Skills for All Ages Book 1: Basic Life Skills covers skills so simple most emergency preparedness books skip right over them. In true emergencies, knowing how to sharpen kitchen knives and basic sanitation can be literal life savers. Skills were chosen for their value in everyday life as well as emergencies.

Survival Skills for All Ages Book 2: 52⁺ Recipes for Everyday & Emergencies is full of simple recipes that can be cooked on or off-grid, so you can serve normal meals even without power, and recipes for staples such as mayonnaise, baking powder, and crackers.

Survival Skills for All Ages Book 3: 26 Mental & Urban Life Skills covers financial skills, staying safe while traveling, self-defense, cyber security, hiding from danger, handling your emotions (including stress and anger), and more. These skills can help kids and adults throughout life, not just in emergencies.

The Organized Wedding: Planning Everything from Your Engagement to Your Marriage is chock full of checklists. No detail is too small! What truly sets it apart is including the actual wedding ceremony and a chapter on your marriage with questions on financial priorities, family health history, and all your doctors.

OMG! Not the Zombies! Book 1 A group of teens goes for a hike and accidentally starts the zombie apocalypse. Being good at being prepared, they start setting up a safe community in the old Indian cliff houses and stocking it with supplies to save themselves and their families while the adults are still pretending life is normal.

BRB! Not the Zombies! Book 2 As their group grows, they discover a new mission: Get crucial information and items to the CDC to help with efforts to create a cure for the Infection. They fight their way through zombie-infested towns and to find the "impregnable" CDC research station their hopes are pinned on.

YOLO! Not the Zombies! Book 3 Have you ever wondered how a hurricane might affect the zombie apocalypse? Or how undead would fare in a sandstorm? (Hint: Hope they aren't wearing a helmet.) These and other natural disasters are explored in these zombie short stories.

Works in Progress:

Survival Skills for All Ages: 26 Outdoor Life Skills covers basic camping skills such as knot tying, fire building, outdoor cooking, and choosing a tent. It also covers hunting, fishing, and foraging for food; finding your way using maps, compasses, and GPSs; and truly basic skills such as managing time and water safety (tides, currents, etc.).

Survival Skills for All Ages: Special Needs Prepping may sound like something only "other people" need but the truth is that most families have special needs. Babies, elderly parents, diabetes, asthma, allergies—most of us have at least one of these and even if we don't, a simple sprained ankle or back injury can make us (temporarily) special needs.

Contact the Author

Bethanne Kim would love to hear from you! She maintains two blogs. The Moderate Mom focuses on politics. Wise Fathers avoids politics.

You can connect with her through:

    Email–theWiseMom@WiseFathers.com

    Blogs–TheModerateMom.com; WiseFathers.com

    Facebook–The Moderate Mom; Wise Fathers

    Pinterest–TheModerateMom; WiseFathers

    Twitter–@TheModerateMom; @Wisefatherss

Because Amazon reviews really do matter, especially for indie authors, please take a few minutes and post a review of this book on Amazon.com.